Hiring Top
TALENT

For Sales & Customer Service

by Carl Henry

© 2009 Carl Henry. All rights reserved. Printed and bound in the United States of America. No part of this book my be reproduced or transmitted in any form or by any means, electronic or mechanical, including photocopying, recording, or by an information storage and retrieval system − except by a reviewer who may quote brief passages in a review to be printed in a magazine, newspaper, or on the Web − without permission in writing from the author. For information, please contact Henry Associates, 9430 Valley Road, Charlotte, NC 28270.

Cover Design by Alex LaFasto
Book design by Nichole Ward, Morrison Alley Design

Although the author and publisher have made every effort to ensure the accuracy and completeness of information contained in this book, we assume no responsibility for errors, inaccuracies, omissions, or any inconsistency herein. Any slights of people, places, or organizations are unintentional.

First Printing 2009

ISBN-13   978-0-9817915-2-4

For Will and Virginia

Contents

	Introduction	x
Chapter 1:	Why You Need Top Talent	1
Chapter 2:	Who's Available	7
Chapter 3:	What Is Top Talent	13
Chapter 4:	Finding Top Talent	19
Chapter 5:	Hiring Mistakes Are Expensive	27
Chapter 6:	The Three-Legged Hiring Stool	33
Chapter 7:	How To Train And Motivate Top Talent	41
Chapter 8:	Inherited Employees	47
Chapter 9:	The Hiring Mindset	53

INTRODUCTION

Which would you rather have, a map leading to buried treasure, or a description of what's inside? If you answered "both," you're in good company. For the past several years, I've been consulting for a number of clients on hiring salespeople, customer service professionals, and other staff. For the most part, I've kept to helping them identify employees and prospects who have the skills and talents to be superstars in their profession. When it comes to searching for top talent, though, my clients have been on their own; my standard answer has been "I don't know where you find them, but I can tell you if they're any good."

As it turns out, that answer isn't good enough. Hiring is one of the most important, if not *the* most important, parts of a manager's job. Without a quality team working around you, it's impossible to get ahead. Big goals become minor ongoing struggles and efficiency suffers. And yet, many of the otherwise sharp and ambitious professionals I work with routinely settle for bringing "warm bodies" into their offices and facilities. They look to their one or two top producers – the key members of their staff who they can count on to get things done – with a wishful eye. "If only I could have a few more like them," they say, "we could really get something done."

The good news here is that you *can* find more like them. In fact, there are ambitious men and women in every city, every country, and every industry where people do business. There are literally millions of people across every age and experience level who can step in and make a difference in what you're doing. The bad news, however, is that they aren't always going to be easy to find. What's worse, you'll have to weed through lots of other folks who look like superstars, but aren't. And even when you find the right person, you'll need to fight to keep them. It's not going to be easy, but that's the reality of today's business world.

Besides, it's well worth the trouble. Once you realize how to find and keep top talent, you'll wonder how you ever got by before. Hiring the best person for each job is by far the fastest way to improve your company or department.

So, let's take the problem head on. I'll agree to stop dodging the question of where to find new hires, and what to do with them, if you'll agree to only bring in the best. In this short book, we'll walk through all the steps of the hiring process, including searching for fresh faces, evaluating candidates, training and motivating your new employees, and even evaluating the costs of a hiring mistake. Along the way, you won't just see why your hiring decisions are so important, you'll also see how you can improve them right away.

Hiring well is the hallmark of great manager. Nothing else you can do has so much potential to improve the profitability of your company or department while decreasing your stress at the same time. Let's get started…

> **Top talent is the one** *edge in your business that can't be* **duplicated by your competitors.**

CHAPTER ONE
Why You Need Top Talent

If you're a manager picking up this book for the first time, and you've just flipped through the table of contents, you might be wondering why I'm making such a big deal about hiring top talent. After all, finding superstars is great, but there are only so many of them to go around. Besides, chances are that your company has done pretty well for itself using your current interview and selection process. So why worry about it?

To answer that, I'd like to tell you a little story. A few times a year I attend various trade shows. Sometimes, I do it to touch base with my biggest clients, or to keep tabs with what's going on in different industries. Other times, I just want to see what's new. No matter what the reason for my trip, however, I'm always amazed at the fresh innovations that are constantly coming to market. Over the past twenty years, I've seen more new inventions, technologies, and improvements than I would have ever thought possible.

As amazing as some companies have been in coming up with new ideas, though, their competitors have been just as impressive in their ability to adapt. As quickly as something can be thought of and produced, someone else can come in and copy the same thing, or even improve upon it. In other words, nothing stays new forever. Whatever great new idea or product you launched today, everyone else will be selling tomorrow. I've seen it time and time again, at shows across North America and around the world. In fact, it's gotten to where I can almost count on it; if I see something really great one year, I know I'll be seeing it again a dozen more times the next year.

Given the harsh reality that no product stays protected or innovative for very long, how is it that some companies manage to stay ahead of the competition? The answer, in a word, is *people*. No matter how closely someone copies a product or process, they're doing just that, copying. In other words, they can duplicate the thing, but not the creativity or hard work behind it. More often than not, it's not the product itself, but the superior sales and customer service that attracted buyers in the first place. And so, when clients look to buy, who do you think they turn to?

In any business, having an edge when it comes to employees and team members will always be decisive. It's the one part of your business that can't be copied, borrowed, stolen, or undercut by price. And the biggest ingredient in your staff's success is *talent* – having the right people for the right jobs.

This is an area where many managers and executives become confused. That's because most people have a tendency to confuse talent with skills. Both are important, but the second never matters if you don't have the first. A salesperson who doesn't have some natural level of ability isn't likely to make his quotas, much less become a superstar. Likewise, a customer service rep who doesn't have a gift for working with people stands very little chance of doing anything more than aggravating clients and collecting a check.

And yet, it's not unusual for me to talk to managers who claim that they could get more out of their staff if they only had the proper training or motivational tools. This is like saying you could ride your lawnmower in the Daytona 500 if only you used better gas; in both cases, you weren't starting out with the right material. No amount of tweaking or teaching is going to do a lot to change it.

My friend and colleague Bill Bonnstetter estimates that a good three quarters of all people are in the wrong jobs. This disconnect between talent and fit is a major problem, for both employers and employees. From management's perspective, there are always a small group of folks who do their jobs and do them well. Recognizing this, managers spend untold amounts of time and money trying to get their other employees to match this output. This is almost always an impossibility, though, because these people didn't have the right tools to start with.

From the other side, things are just as bad. Employees who aren't a good fit for their jobs quickly become burnt out and disengaged. Sometimes they try to keep their frustrations to themselves, but it's usually obvious to everyone that they aren't that interested in their work. What's more, they resent being compared to the top performers, which makes further training a waste of time and money. These people are square pegs trying to fit in round holes; pushing them harder isn't going to do much good.

Despite the major effort that most companies undertake to move the immovable, most of us realize how important top talent is. It's easy to see that some people have a certain spark in them; they work harder because their job is a good reflection of their own abilities and motivations. We love working with them because they always go the extra mile. They're so good at their jobs that they make ours easier, too, and we're always wishing we had more like them.

Why is it, then, that we don't make more of an effort to find these superior performers to fill job openings? The easiest answer, I suppose, is that it's hard work. It's not like there's an ad you can place or an agency you can go to that can match the perfect person for every job. No, finding the right man or woman means long hours scanning resumes and sitting through interviews. Still, I think most managers would gladly trade the extra hours for a top-notch staff.

The second reason could be that many managers just don't know where to look. Almost everybody looks good on a resume or during an interview, so picking out the real winners can be a chore. This is another big problem, and one we'll look at later, but I don't think it's the biggest one, either.

I think the single biggest reason most managers end up with mediocre employees is that they hire for the wrong reasons. That is, they bring someone in because they need "a fresh body." Or, they've been told by an owner or executive to grow the company, fill a spot, or put another pin in the map. In each case, the pressure to fill the position is greater than the desire to fill it with the right person. The temptation to move quickly seems justified. After all, isn't having someone who's not perfect better than having no one at all? The answer to that question is almost always a resounding "no," and that kind of thinking could be costing you tens of thousands of dollars every year. Hiring because you need someone is almost always a terrible idea, and it's the biggest reason employers settle for mediocre players when they should be looking for top talent.

Keep that in mind as you look through the rest of these pages. Finding people is no place to skimp on time, money, or effort. Hiring the right team doesn't make a difference; it makes *all* the difference. Talent is the one thing you need to stay ahead, and it's the one thing you can't buy or train.

> *To jump start your organization, you must find top talent.*

CHAPTER TWO
Who's Available?

Before we get into the best ways to find and identify top talent, it makes sense to take a minute to talk about who is available. That's because today's managers don't have to deal just with resumes and qualifications, they need to bring in new people in an environment where the demographics are undergoing major shifts.

These changes are easy to see. The baby boomers, those of us born in the years following the end of World War II, have been the face of the American workforce for a long time. Around 80 million children were born in this period after the war ended, making us an economic tidal wave. Not only did our sheer numbers put us at the forefront, but as a whole we've been working longer, more productively, and with more tools at our disposal than any generation that came before us. In fact, one of the most striking characteristics of our generation has been the tendency to put off retirement until later in life, opting instead for second and third careers.

Because of this, the management and ownership of many companies is dominated by the boomer generation. Nor is it unusual to find us at the head of nonprofits and civic organizations. More and more of us, rather than golfing in Florida, are deciding that we'd like to continue making impacts either in the business world or for our favorite causes.

But time doesn't stand still forever. And while we're working longer than our parents did, that doesn't mean we can't appreciate the joys of working less, or not at all. And so, as we retire, younger generations have been taking our place. The next in line, of course, is the famously named "Generation X." These younger people, (born between the 1960s and 1980s, depending on who you ask) were viewed with suspicion for a long time by my generation. Much smaller than the boomers, representing just over half of our size, they were brought up in a time when the world was changing, and so they picked up new attitudes and work habits. Specifically, they are more technology-oriented than the boomers, and more likely to pick up on unconventional ideas.

Maybe for that reason, Gen X'ers were feared to be slackers who wouldn't put in the hard work needed to drive business forward. The reality, though, has been that they've done as well as anyone else – just in their own way. By looking "outside the box," they've embraced a lot of ideas and solutions that weren't even imaginable – much less in existence – when we were younger. The result has been new industries: there are more jobs and profits in internet ventures than there are in the automobile industry.

Finally, there's the newest batch, Generation Y, also known as Echo boomers, or Millennials. They've embraced this greater sense of technology that started with their parents and run with it. In a word, they're "wired." Their computer isn't just a tool, it's a part of the lifestyle that they use to network, find information, and stay in touch with the world around them. Nobody knows much about this group in the workforce, since most of them are in college or just entering their first jobs. But they represent a huge market for employers (they number almost as many as the baby boomers did), so you can be sure we'll be finding out a lot about them soon.

And even for domestic companies, the job market doesn't end there. The United States is currently home to nearly 40 million legal immigrants, the largest number anywhere in the world. While the subject of who should be allowed in and who shouldn't always makes for a hot political topic, the fact of the matter is that it comes down to simple math. In other words, we have more jobs than we have people. Importing talent is a great way for us to stay competitive. And naturally, if you have operations overseas, as many of my clients do, then you'll be able to tap into the vast numbers of foreign workers that are out there.

So what's the point in all of this? Why should we bother knowing how many millions of men and women there are in one generation, or how they work? The answer is simple – this knowledge can give you a competitive advantage.

The world is stuffed full of competent, talented people who can push your company forward, but you have to be willing to look for them, and not just in the places you expect to find them. Too many managers remain stuck in their thinking when it comes to finding new people. There are boomer generation supervisors who don't want to hire Generation X'ers, and vice versa, even though it could be exactly what their departments need.

Think about it this way: if you have twenty people working for you, what are the odds that you're better off with all of them having the same background and viewpoint? Not very good. The best teams I know of have a mixture – some folks with experience, others who bring fresh ideas, a couple that have seen the way people do things in other places, and one or two that understand what's going on with new technologies.

In short, I'm telling you to break out of your shell and look around. Lots of companies are investing in diversity training these days, and that's great. But my advice isn't based on the greater good – it's about the bottom line. Having different kinds of people around means you can sell more and deliver better service, so don't be afraid to look past the very basics when you hire.

So, who's available? Everbody. Now, let's take a look at how you find them.

> **Top Talent can** *revolutionize your company. It's more important than capital, technology, or even your brand name.*

CHAPTER THREE

What Is Top Talent?

For all the trouble we're making over hiring top talent, you might be wondering, "what exactly *is* top talent?" Unfortunately, there's no one set answer. That's because every company and industry is different; there are no apples to apples comparisons. While a superstar furniture salesperson might move several pieces every day, a top performer in heavy machinery could be outselling his peers by closing one sale every quarter.

Even so, I think we can set out some reasonable guidelines. For instance, in sales, I like to say that a top performer is someone who out-produces his or her counterparts by four to five times every month. In other words, if your average salesperson brings in around $10,000 in new business each week, then a superstar will probably bring in $40,000 or $50,000. Of course, those numbers might not be relevant in your industry – the average might be much greater or smaller – but you get the idea; a superstar salesperson is adding a hefty chunk to your bottom line.

Those numbers point to a major reason why sales managers tend to pick up on this concept quickly. When you realize that having the right salesperson can gain you four to five times income or more in each territory you operate, it starts to make sense to bring in top talent as quickly and as often as you can.

On the customer service side, things get a little murkier. In most cases, the performance of customer care reps can't always be evaluated strictly by the numbers, since they aren't working on a commission basis. Beyond the parts and service sales they generate, you might have a hard time tying their work to your quarterly profits. This isn't to say that they don't contribute in this area; your sales force might open the account, but it's often going to be up to your customer service staff to generate subsequent orders. The most successful organizations are sales-driven, so it's crucial that your frontline employees do everything they can to bring in new business.

At the same time, there are some standards by which we can evaluate customer care staff. One of the most obvious is complaints. Every customer service professional, no matter how strong or talented, is going to face a small percentage of customers that they can't please. For whatever reason – perhaps because they were treated rudely by another employee, or received a severely defective product – these folks are going to be hostile and eventually end up wanting to speak with a manager.

But by keeping track of how many complaints are angry customers a specific rep passes on, you can form a picture of how effectively they are doing their job. Another way to measure their performance is by keeping track of how many calls or inquiries each person handles. A more efficient and engaged professional will almost always serve a greater number of customers. You could also take a look at how many refunds, discounts, or other incentives they're giving away. If you have someone who constantly throws money at customers just to get them off the phone or out of the office, then they're obviously not saving you as much money as someone who finds more creative ways to resolve situations.

In order for you to make use of any of these guidelines, however, you have to keep good track of what's going on with your team. Some managers I meet do a fantastic job of this, and can tell you precisely how many calls each person on their staff handles, how long they take with each one, and what the ultimate resolution is. Other supervisors do very little in the way of record-keeping and follow-up. This may save time in the short term, but how can they know who's doing the hard work on their teams? If you want to have top talent, you need to know who they are. Keeping good notes and records is a step in that direction.

Also notice how your new hires are working with others. One of the easiest ways to spot top talent in employees is by studying the way their peers interact with them. If they're liked and respected, then there's a good chance they're producing quality work. On the other hand, if the rest of your staff tends to exclude somebody, or work around them, then you should ask yourself why. Do they routinely miss deadlines? Are they not pulling their own weight? The answers should be easy to get to, but only if you're leading your team in a hands-on way. In order to have a sense of what's going on with your staff, you need to be working closely with them.

That being said, though, these guidelines are most useful in large departments, or in cases where you have new employees. That's because top talent is a bit like fine art; it's easy to spot when you're looking at it, even if you can't exactly explain why. For as much as top performers do, they're just as noticeable for the things they *don't do*. Rarely will one of the superstars on your staff miss work for no reason, or cause problems with other employees. Likewise, they won't usually take up a lot of your time with personal problems, or need to be micromanaged. That's because these people are internally driven and motivated; they don't need your direction or encouragement to work hard.

Make no mistake – this is a bigger point than most managers think. You might be driven to seek top talent by the desire for higher profit margins or lower turnover costs, but once your staff can function and thrive without consuming every bit of your energy and attention, you'll wonder how you ever got along without people that work that way. Having a team that can carry out your instructions, and work smoothly when you're not around, frees you up to run your department or company in a way that makes sense. Gone are the days lost to sorting out internal squabbles, or trying to get people moving. In their place are profitable weeks and quarters carving out new markets and making your business run more efficiently. Most of the managers I know are extremely busy. They don't need to spend their days mentoring and fostering someone who's going to do an average job and soak up a lot of their attention. Wouldn't you rather have someone who can take the initiative to get things done on his or her own?

As I'll say many times in this book, having a great team makes all the difference. So take these guidelines and decide what they mean to your business. How many sales, or what kind of attitude, does it take to be a superstar on your team? Keep those answers in the back of your mind, and you'll learn to spot top talent when it comes along.

> **The key to finding**
> *top talent isn't where...*
> *it's when.*

CHAPTER FOUR

Finding Top Talent

Health experts will tell you that you should never walk into a grocery store when you're hungry. Why? Because you're bound to walk out with a lot more than you need. It might seem counterintuitive, but we've all been there. When you're dying to grab something to eat, those packages seem like they're screaming from the shelves. You've got a deep, sudden craving – for everything. And so, giving in to the urges, you grab a few boxes of this, and a couple more cans of that. Sometimes, they're foods you wouldn't even normally want, and won't end up eating until the next time you've missed a meal.

Even worse, you're far more likely to pick up junk food than you are to choose food that's nutritious. Your body, still programmed to hunt for berries and run from mammoths, sees your hunger as a threat of oncoming starvation. Its natural response is to ask you for foods that leave you with some reserves to spare. More often than not, that means ice cream, sausage pizza, or a good old bacon cheeseburger.

Believe it or not, this is actually a fantastic analogy to the art of hiring. You see, now that we've made a couple of important points about who's available, it's time to get into the heart of the matter – where to find top talent. As I mentioned before, this is an issue of supreme importance to managers, and one I avoided answering for a long time. But after taking a good look at how the best managers find their top performers, I've come to realize that the secret isn't in the where; it's in the *when*. And the answer, for those who truly want to hire top talent, is *always*.

That's because looking for a new employees is a lot like looking for new customers. If you're always doing it, then you stand a pretty good chance of always having somebody new with which to work. But, if you wait until the last minute – when your stomach is growling and you absolutely have to make something happen – then you're likely be disappointed. One reason is the time available. Searching for a new hire when you need someone means doing it quickly; there's less time for scouting and interviewing than you might otherwise devote. Another more important factor is pressure. The worst time to find a new employee is when you need one, because every day that you don't have somebody means lost sales or decreased productivity. So, the tendency in that situation is to hire the first person who seems at all close to what you're looking for, just so you can get the position filled.

With that in mind, don't think of recruiting as something you do quarterly, periodically, or when you have a job opening. Train yourself to do it constantly. Even if you can only devote an hour a week to looking for fresh faces, start doing it. It doesn't matter how many openings you have, or how many you don't. Just make a point of getting out there to look for top talent. Where should you start?

One obvious place to look is within your own staff. People tend to know other people who are a lot like themselves. In fact, if you think within your own circle of friends, I'd be willing to bet you can think of more than a couple that share a similar background, experience level, and work ethic with you. It's the same with your staff. If you have a good team, and need a few more just like them, asking them for referrals is a good place to start. In the same way, your customers can be a good source of new names. If you have worked with someone for many years, and trust their opinion, why not ask if they know someone?

You could also check out your competitors. In many industries, it's not uncommon for companies to bring in retreads, that is, sales or customer service people coming from other firms in the same industry. Be careful with these, though. On the surface, hiring them makes a lot of sense. After all, how can you do any better than somebody who already knows your industry, product, and territory? Lots of managers, having these thoughts, will hire their competitors' staff with a lot less scrutiny than they'd give somebody off the street. But more often than not, this is a mistake.

When someone, especially in sales, decides to find a new employer, you have to ask yourself why. A superstar salesperson at any firm will already be making a lot of money and have a pretty big customer base. So why would they want to change that? Granted, there are some legitimate reasons they might look to make a move. But it's more likely that they're looking for a fresh start because things haven't panned out at their first company. Most managers recognize this, at least on some level, but overlook it because they want to jumpstart their sales. And indeed, these folks very frequently come with promises of existing accounts and new leads that can be closed right away. Again, though, ask yourself: why haven't they closed this new business already? And what's kept them from success at their old company? Often the answer is attitude. What will make your company any different for them? Think long and hard on the answers to these questions before hiring someone from a competing firm.

The same caution applies to bringing in customer service staff from other companies. Why, after taking the time to learn someone else's products and policies, are they willing and eager to start over? What opportunities do you offer that they couldn't get elsewhere? If you can't find good answers to these questions, be wary of hiring someone and expecting them to become top performers just because they supposedly know your business.

On the other side of the spectrum from retreads, I meet lots of managers who avoid, or outright refuse, to hire people that come to them through headhunters. They figure that after the headhunters' commission is figured in, these people will be too expensive. On the one hand, I'm inclined to agree. Everybody knows that middlemen increase costs, and it's no different with labor than anything else. However, I would point out that the right person is the right person, regardless of how they come to you. The best thing you can do for yourself is bring in top talent, even if it costs you a little more. We're going to take a look at the high costs of turnover – and they're higher than you think – but for now, I just want to point out that you're much better paying a decent salary and a headhunter's commission than you are hiring the wrong person, paying them a salary and benefits while they don't work out, and then going through the whole thing all over again.

These days, the Internet can be another great source of new hiring leads. Sites like monster.com and careerbuilder.com are virtual clearinghouses of new talent, as are the hundreds of local community pages and job boards. Of course, the downside of any kind of online search is the high number of responses – mostly from people who aren't qualified or a good fit – that you have to go through to find suitable candidates. Still, the same caveats apply to traditional off-line methods, like newspaper or magazine ads, and at least you can narrow your criteria online. Regardless of where you place an ad, whether it's online or offline, know that it's a game of percentages. In other words, you're probably going to spend a lot of time sifting through the responses before you find the person you're looking for.

Besides, these are just the obvious places. As I mentioned before, the best managers are always looking for fresh faces. That means that they've got their eyes open all of the time, even when they're away from normal recruiting channels. For instance, one manager I know hired a performer he saw at a local theater production. The young man showed great delivery and instincts throughout his performance. Toward the end, the supervisor thought, "Wow, this person could be great in sales." So, he talked to him after the show, and the rest is history. Another hired her package delivery man to work in her customer service department, because she recognized in him a talent for dealing with people.

These are just a couple of examples, but the point is that you run into potential superstar salespeople or customer service agents in your everyday life. The problem is, you're not thinking about hiring, so you don't notice them. Then, when the time comes to get somebody, you're starting from scratch. You always have to have your eyes and ears open. Your campaign to find top talent should be ongoing.

Let me say it again: you should be looking for talented employees all the time, even if you don't have any openings, or don't expect to have any in the near future. It's better to have one or two superstars on staff, even if you haven't figured out a permanent place for them, then it is to need one urgently and settle for hiring a warm body. If you don't have that luxury, then you should at the very least keep a file of candidates that you think might be great for some spot in your company or department in the future. You don't have to take a great deal of time with it, just keep growing your list and check in with people from time to time and see what they're up to. By giving it that small bit of effort, you can jump way ahead of the curve when it comes to filling open jobs with the most talented people around.

Having an ongoing recruiting effort is something that pays huge dividends over time. To see how, just imagine that tomorrow morning one of your very best employees said they were leaving. Now imagine, instead of feeling stressed and wondering how your department would survive without them, you feel the security that comes from having three or four really strong candidates ready to take their place. That's the power of continuous recruiting, and you should have it working for you and your company.

> **Poor hiring decisions**
> *cost more in time, energy, and money*
> *than you think.*

CHAPTER FIVE
Hiring Mistakes Are Expensive

One of the easiest ways to make more money is to waste less of it, so it's no surprise that most of today's managers have also become expert cost-cutters. From office supplies to travel budgets, top supervisors routinely find ways to get more from less. That's why I've been so shocked to learn how few of them realize the true cost of a hiring mistake.

Like utility bills or postage expenses, lots of supervisors I talk to view turnover as just another "cost of doing business." What they don't realize, though, is that these costs can easily run out of control. Consider for a moment what happens whenever there's an opening to be filled. First, the very fact that someone needs to be hired means that some area of work probably isn't being taken care of; there's a job that isn't being done. This might be unavoidable – employees move, retire, and leave your company for dozens of reasons. Even so, keep in mind that an opening represents work that needs to be done. Whether it ends up being finished by you, other members of your staff, temporary employees, or the person who is ultimately hired full-time doesn't matter, because each of these represents a cost to your company or department.

Of course, those costs are miniscule compared to what you'll spend bringing in someone new. But before you can even consider that, you have to round up some candidates. This usually means placing ads, either online or in the newspaper, or attending job fairs and trade shows. Each of these costs money, and bring yet another task — digging through piles of resumes. To find four or five qualified candidates from the stack of responses you'll likely get takes time. I don't think it's a stretch to say that most of the managers I work with are short on available hours. So in essence, they're throwing away their most valuable resource looking for the needle in the haystack.

After the resumes have been reviewed and a few likely prospects picked out, the interviews can begin. It usually takes two or three good interviews to narrow down the field and decide on someone, which means more time is being burned, including hours spent on the men and women who won't be hired. You can also figure in airfare, hotels, and meals if you're considering candidates from other areas.

Assuming that the interviews have gone well, you're finally ready to hire someone. This is where the expenses start to really add up. You might have spent a minor fortune on ads, travel, and lost productivity looking for your new employee, but that's nothing compared to what you'll burn now if they don't work out. The most obvious expense is your new employee's salary, which you'll probably pay for six months to a year, in the best case. Besides that, you'll also be on the hook for their benefits, which run many companies a full fifty percent more than a staff member's base pay.

You might still be thinking that these costs aren't *so bad*, considering that you now have someone filling the position. Keep in mind, though, that it takes most new employees at least a few months to become integrated into the department and generate any real productivity. It's also likely that you'll spend much of this time training them, either with other employees who could be working elsewhere or through materials that have to be continually updated at a cost. Getting new people up to speed isn't cheap, but there's no way around it if you hope to ever earn a return on your investment.

Finally, after a few months, your new hire should start being productive. But what if they aren't? What if they don't buy into your company's philosophy, aren't highly motivated, or just prove to be a bad fit for the position? At this point, you're faced with two unappealing prospects: either starting the whole process over again, or keeping an employee (and salary) that isn't doing you much good. Obviously, if you're forced to do the first, then you've wasted a good deal of time and money. What's more, because you're likely to sorely need a new face now, you'll probably be even less discriminating with your next hire, meaning that it's just as likely you'll end up with an underperformer.

I suspect that lost time and money is why many supervisors go with the second route – keeping the employee in place. But I would argue that such a strategy is likely to cost you even more over the long run, and here's why: having someone who isn't engaged or isn't a team player working for you brings down everyone with which you do business. Other employees are frustrated at the employee's lack of enthusiasm or productivity, customers get tired of dealing with someone who isn't competent, and your ideas and policies can't be carried out effectively.

In sales, I call this territory destruction. Simply put, it's the loss that comes with having people who can't, or won't, do their jobs the right way, which inevitably creates a negative impression of your company. The worst part is, you probably won't realize how bad the problem is until it's too late. Once in a while, an employee will perform so poorly that a customer, vendor, or other associate will actually call or contact the manager to complain. Everybody hates to get these calls, but they're much better than the alternative. In many cases, people won't tell you how bad a person was until after they've already left. They might not speak up because they don't want to ruin their relationship with you. Or, it could be that they don't want to endure an uncomfortable discussion with your employee. Either way, they simply keep their feelings to themselves – that is, until the employee has left your company, along with the other employees and customers who didn't wait around to see the bad apple dropped.

There's no way around it, hiring mistakes are very, very expensive. The best way to keep your costs down and morale up is to spend the time and effort bringing in the right person the first time. In the next chapter, we'll look at what I call the "three-legged stool of hiring," which is a system designed to help you examine job candidates in a way that makes sense.

"*To be truely successful*
       in evaluating potential employees,
you need a plan."

CHAPTER SIX
The Three-Legged Hiring Stool

To those in the know, my current home of North Carolina is one of the furniture capitals of the world. Numerous sofa and cabinet makers call the area home, sending their products to stores and ultimately homes all over the world. I've never built anything like that myself, but when I pass the factories and showrooms, I'm always reminded of my grandfather.

When I was still a small boy, my mother would sometimes drive us out to see him on a weekend or a holiday. Besides the things most kids remember about grandparents, like candy and presents, the thing that I recall most is his workshop. Whenever we'd show up, he'd come out from there and greet us, having been busy shaping a chair or some other project. I wouldn't be able to name half the things he put together in there, but I do remember watching him put together a stool one Saturday afternoon. He was already working when I woke up, and for hours I sat by while he put the pieces together.

Now, to most people, including my then-young self, a stool seems like a pretty simple project. There's a place to sit, and a couple of legs. How hard could that really be? But as my grandfather spent hours shaping it, I noticed that he went over each leg in fine detail. Finally, I asked him why it was taking so long. He went on to explain something that I still cherish as a great lesson, not only in building, but in life – and as it turns out, hiring.

You see, what my grandfather told me that day was that a stool was a simple thing, but only if all the parts fit together well. That is, you couldn't just rush through it. The seat had to be sturdy, of course, but more importantly, the legs had to be strong. A weakness in one of them, or an uneven length, would make the stool unsteady. Over time, even a small imperfection would break it, often at a moment when someone was sitting comfortably.

I'm bringing this up because it can help us to understand the steps in finding a superstar employee. At this point, you might be so worried about the cost of a hiring mistake that you're starting to wonder if it's worth taking a chance on anyone. After all, if three quarters of the working population are in the wrong job, and it's so hard to find the right person, then what sense does it make to keep bringing in new employees?

Obviously, there's the matter of need. It's impossible to manage and grow any business without bringing in new people, especially in a world where many workers expect to have several careers over their productive lifetimes. A better reason, though, is the one I've stated all along: that there's a small army of talented men and women out there who can make an enormous impact on your organization. All you have to do is find them.

To help in that department, I'd like to suggest you try out what I call my three-legged stool of hiring. It might not be the fanciest name, but it's a handy way of remembering the three tools – resumes, interviews, and hiring assessments – that any manager should turn to before bringing a new employee on to their staff.

As I mentioned, the first is a good old-fashioned resume. There are a lot of problems with resumes, and I'll get to those in a moment, but I still feel like they're a good starting point for any candidate you consider. That's because, in one or two pages, you can see all the basic information about your candidates – like their education, work experience, and job skills – that you need to decide if they're qualified for an interview.

The biggest problem with resumes, of course, is that they *only* give you basic information. Just because somebody went to a good school or held a job for a few years doesn't mean they're going to be a superstar employee. At the same time, lots of resumes contain information that is exaggerated, or outright false. Different studies show that a shockingly high percentage of all resumes out there list education, skills, or other qualifications that simply aren't true.

I had always heard horror stories about lies on resumes, but it didn't really hit home for me until I went to visit a client in India. I was on site to work with his group for just under a week, so we had plenty of time to talk about his new facility and the local talent pool. I was shocked when he mentioned that fraud, especially when it came to degrees that hadn't actually been earned, was rampant throughout the country. Since then, though, I've learned that this is a widespread problem around the globe. It doesn't matter if you have a billion people looking for work or just a few dozen; they're probably going to exaggerate their resumes if they think it will help them get hired.

In addition to the outright lies, job seekers find numerous ways to exaggerate their qualifications. For example, many will include statements like "I increased the sales in my territory five times over in three years." What they aren't telling you is that the rest of their team grew their sales by twenty times, or that company accountants changed the way revenue was calculated. The point is, you can't always trust what's written on someone's resume, even if it seems specific.

Because resumes offer such limited information and aren't a good barometer of how well the candidate will work out, lots of managers place more emphasis on the interview. In general, this is a good strategy. A resume a little more than a piece of paper, while the interview puts a live candidate right across from you. By asking direct questions and getting not only their answers, but a sense of who they are, you can make a much better decision about how likely somebody is to succeed in the job.

As any experienced manager can tell you, though, interviews aren't everything. There are plenty of people who will show up and give you all the right answers to your questions, yet still disappoint you after you actually hire them. It could be that they just wanted a job, or maybe something about the interview made them seem like a stronger candidate than they actually were. Either way, you have to be careful with interviews, because you won't always get the same person you see.

Keep in mind that that last point mainly applies to those prospective employees who give you a really *good* interview. I know plenty of managers who are inclined to give someone who does poorly in an interview the benefit of the doubt. Either because of a particularly strong resume or some other qualifications, they just assume that the person was having an "off day" and will do better once they actually begin the job. In my experience, this is rarely, if ever, the case. Most people show up to interviews with the new suit and a fresh haircut; they want very badly to put their best foot forward. In other words, an interview often represents your potential new employee at their best. They aren't likely to become more polished or focused once they actually have the job. Keep that in mind as you interview candidates; they're trying to sell you on hiring them, so you should expect to see them at the top of their game.

Even with all the problems that exist with resumes and interviews, a surprising number of supervisors stop there. Doesn't it make sense to find out as much as you can about potential employees (a huge investment for any company) as you can? I think so. And that's why I recommend that everyone use hiring assessments to check out the men and women they are thinking about adding to their teams.

What is a hiring assessment? Basically, it's a short profile that you have a candidate fill out. The whole process takes very little time, and can give you more insight into a person's motivation, personality, and talents than you'd learn in a few years on the job. Put another way, it's a quick, scientific way of finding out what makes them tick. And, combined with the information you get from the resume and series of interviews, you can drastically improve your odds of finding top talent for your open position.

Assessments aren't new, but they've come a long way in the last few decades. It absolutely amazes me that, in this day and age, anyone would think of hiring without them. The risks and rewards involved in bringing in new people are just too great. So if you're seriously considering hiring someone, make the extra effort to find out who they really are before you've invested thousands of dollars in salary, benefits, and training.

Even with assessments, you're still going to make mistakes. Some people just look like top talent, even though they eventually end up being average or poor employees.

That's just part of hiring people, and it will probably be a long time before we'll ever come up with a way to completely eliminate it. In the meantime, though, try out the three-legged hiring stool of resumes, interviews, and assessments. It's not perfect, but it will tilt the odds of finding top talent heavily in your favor.

> **The best employees don't** *need to be motivated, just pointed* **in the right direction.**

CHAPTER SEVEN
How To Train And Motivate Top Talent

Through my son and his friends, I often have the opportunity to observe young people in their natural habitat. Besides making me nostalgic for my own youth, these moments can yield interesting insights that speak to larger issues in life and business. I had one of those moments not long ago, as I watched some high school kids preparing for a track meet.

At first glance, the scene wasn't that remarkable. As the different teams filtered on and around the field, they went about jogging and stretching. But a closer look revealed something interesting – you could frequently guess who would win at the different events, before they'd even begun. This wasn't because certain teens were bigger or smaller than their peers, or because their uniforms or shoes were any different. No, it was because they showed up ready to go. While their peers were chatting away, or retying their laces, these kids looked like *they couldn't wait for the race to start.* And sure enough, they almost always took home the prizes.

A high school track meet might not seem like it would have much to do with your office, but the two aren't as different as you might think. That's because you've got some high flyers working for you, and they're ready to go. Once you've gone through all the time and trouble of finding a superstar employee, the last thing you want to do is lose them. Not only are you out the time and expense of any new hire that doesn't work out, but you're also back to square one when it comes to filling the position. Talented workers are the proverbial needle in a haystack; managers should take special care to avoid dropping them back into the pile.

It's easier to do than you might expect, especially if you aren't used to working with top talent. That's because they want to get off to a fast start. While your average employee might want to spend days, weeks, or even months training and getting acclimated, superstars want to hit the ground running. With that in mind, don't skimp on training, but don't draw it out, either. Do what you can to get them integrated into their new position rapidly and let them take on new responsibilities. Keeping them away from the action is likely to frustrate them, and you don't want them looking for a more dynamic job before they've even gotten settled into your company.

Also, make sure they have the equipment they need to be productive. You might think that having glitchy computers, enduring unreliable phones, and running out of office supplies are no big deal, but they might send your best employees out the door. Remember, top performers want to do their jobs well; they aren't showing up just to draw a check. If it seems like your company or department isn't up to their standards or ambitions, they'll look for another one that is.

It's also a good idea to pair your new hires with the superstars in your existing staff. That's because you don't want average performers training your next generation of employees and passing on their bad habits. When you put two outstanding talents together, you often get amazing results. On the other hand, even the best new hire will almost always be dragged down by a team of mediocre players working around them, or especially training them. So be sure that your new employees are being brought up by men and women who will encourage them to approach their jobs and careers in the right way.

You probably noticed that much of this comes down to maintaining enthusiasm. And really, that's the secret to keeping top talent. While you might spend a great deal of time and money trying to motivate your average employees, someone who is a top talent won't need that much of a push. That's not to say you should make an effort to keep them happy and engaged, only that you need to recognize that these are folks who are driven for the most part by their own internal desire to be the best. Like track stars getting ready for a race, they've already come to you warmed up and ready to run; all you need to do is give them a fresh pair shoes and point the way.

To that end, nothing beats leading by example. If new employees see you jumping into your job with enthusiasm, they'll likely respond in kind. Remember, excitement is contagious. If you're pumped up about your job, and the rest of your staff is too, that energy will catch on with new people. On the other hand, if you and your team look and act like someone had to drag you out of bed to make it to the office, it won't take long before even the most motivated new employee starts to slow down.

So, be sure the folks around you are having a good time with their jobs. And while you're at it, make sure you are too. It only takes one poor attitude to drag down the morale of any staff, and one of a manager's toughest challenges is keeping whiners, complainers, and other productivity inhibiters out of their office. In fact, I'd go as far as to say that if you have those types of people on your staff, you'd do well to look to replacing them first. Because even though they might be doing their jobs, they're still probably costing you a lot more than they're worth.

Finding top talent is a tough job, but it's worth it in the long run. To reap the benefits, though, you have to put your new star employees in a position to succeed. And that doesn't just mean giving them a desk and a stack of business cards – it means surrounding them with the tools and people that will allow them to shine.

> ***Every company has** employees that never should have been hired in the first place.*

CHAPTER EIGHT

Inherited Employees

If you received a phone call right now, informing you of an unexpected inheritance, what would your first thoughts be? If you're like most of us, you probably imagined untold riches left by a long-lost uncle, or maybe a beach house bequeathed by a forgotten aunt. Chances are, you didn't immediately picture a rundown plot in a backwater town, or a fixer-upper sitting atop a sinking foundation. Realistically, though, your chances are about just as good either way. It's not uncommon for someone to leave something fantastic, but at the same time, not everything you inherit is the windfall you think it is.

It's the same way with inherited employees, those men and women who come under your supervision when you accept a new managerial post or purchase a business. Often, what seems like a gift can end up being a mixed bag. While there might be a few superstar salespeople or customer service professionals on staff, you're also likely to have lots of average employees, along with a few bad apples. So the question is, how should a new manager deal with the staff of inherited employees?

In my line of work, I've seen the good, the bad, and the ugly of these situations. And for the most part, I can tell you that starting off on the right foot is the key to success. You need to establish a culture of winning enthusiasm right away, because without that you're going to be doomed to whatever attitudes and ideas were in place before you showed up. In some cases, that can be a blessing. If the manager that came before you did a fantastic job of working with staff, and only left because they were so successful that they were promoted, then you're probably going to have an easy go of it. On the other hand, and far more commonly, if you're replacing someone who wasn't up to the task, then things might get uglier before they get prettier.

That's because a lazy predecessor can hurt you in a number of ways. For one thing, they've probably left your team with a pile of bad habits. This is noticeable in offices where the staff routinely show up late, take long breaks, and get very little done. There probably has been little or no accountability in the preceding months or years, so there's been no incentive for anyone to push forward. In the same way, you're unlikely to know who the top and bottom performers on your new staff are, since you probably have very little in the way of notes and records. And, to add more fuel to the fire, managers are most often replaced in departments that aren't doing well. So, besides having a poor work ethic and no discipline, your new team is probably low on morale.

One of the quickest ways to turn things around is to set concrete, short-term goals. By giving everybody something immediate to aim for, you can quickly set a new tone around the office. It's important that the goal be reachable, though, for a couple of reasons. First, it helps show your employees that you mean to get things done, but without placing an enormous strain on them. And second, it allows you to see who's up to the task and who isn't. A moderate target will yield three groups on your team – the top performers who will exceed your request, lots of average employees who will meet your request to avoid punishment, and the bottom tier team members who will fail to accomplish much of anything.

Obviously, that first group is what you're looking for. Those are the men and women that you want to keep and develop. Out of the middle group, you might decide to encourage them to make an effort and revisit them later. As for the last group of employees, however – those who aren't productive, or who have poor attitudes – do yourself a favor and replace them as quickly as possible. As I mentioned in the last chapter, few things are as disastrous to your team as having poor performers around, so do what you can to rid yourself of them promptly.

Be aware, though, that there can be heavy legal consequences to this. When dealing with established employees, it's a great idea to consult your legal and human resources departments before making any final decisions. It's an unfortunate reality that lawsuits have become a part of today's business landscape. A previous supervisor might not have held employees to the same standards that you will demand, leaving the possibility that a dismissed worker will claim they were fired for reasons of discrimination. For that reason, it's important to have all of your paperwork in order before you let go a familiar face around the office. As a rule of thumb, the longer someone's been on the job, the more careful you should be in letting them go.

At the same time, don't be in a rush to bring in new faces. Remember, hiring top talent is an ongoing process. There's no shortcut or quick way to do it. Taking over as a manager – especially a new one – often means starting out with what you're given. Get what productivity you can out of your current team, whoever they may be, and then work on adding pieces of the puzzle. The worst thing you can do is bring in a dozen or more fresh faces who have no idea how the company works and mix them in with veteran employees who resent seeing their peers let go. In other words, make changes, but do them at a reasonable pace. Even top talent employees need time to get integrated, so don't add the extra pressure of throwing them all into the fire together at once.

When it comes to inheriting a team of employees, just think long term and work back from there. Unless you're either extremely lucky or unlucky, you're probably going to have a mix of top talent, average employees, and men and women you can't get rid of quickly enough. The trick to making things work is to remember that you need superstar employees, but you're not likely to get them right away. Just follow the advice in this book, keep an open eye for potential winners, and bring them in when it makes sense. It might not be easy, and it might not happen all at once. But once you have a great staff in place, you'll be set to inherit some fantastic things from yourself – a great job, more money, and a better career.

> *Your time is better spent recruiting top talent than it is managing poor performers.*

CHAPTER NINE

The Hiring Mindset

As a business strategist and consultant, I spend a lot of time working closely with my clients around the world. In meetings and over dinners, they tell me about their concerns, and the challenges that are always lurking around the corner. They hire me because they need some new ideas, or an outside perspective on their problems, and I'm thankful for the opportunity to give them those things. And while every situation is a little bit different, I'm often struck by how similar the solutions to various problems can be. I guess I shouldn't be surprised – many of the biggest difficulties in running an organization can be solved with a small, but consistent, effort.

That's how it is with hiring. If you've been in business for more than a month or two, you know how hard it is to find good people. But the answer, unfortunately, isn't in any resume scan or interview question. There's simply no substitute for the hard work of scouting top talent, meeting with them, and then assessing them for the job you want to fill. There are no shortcuts.

But there's good news here. Even though it might be hard to find the right people for your team, if you put in the work, you'll gain a vast advantage over your competitors, and one that they can't steal, buy, or copy. And you'll make things a lot easier – and profitable – for yourself in the process. There's nothing like having a talented, self-motivated staff that runs like a well-oiled engine whether you're around or not.

Just imagine for a moment what it would be like to have a team full of top performers on your payroll, to walk into the office and feel the energy level rise up. How much would it be worth to you to do away with the excuses, absences, missed deadlines, and poor attitudes that come with average and poor employees? I'm betting you'd trade an hour a week to make that happen, and you can.

Remember that the next time you feel like you're too busy to look for new people, or when you're tempted to decide that your staff is "good enough for now." There are literally millions of men and women out there who can make an enormous impact on you, your department, and your company. All you have to do is go and find them.

Hiring top talent is as much a mindset as it is an activity. Make a commitment to yourself that you'll go the extra mile to pass over the warm bodies and find superstars. I can promise you'll be glad you did – *and so will they!*

Carl Henry is a sales educator, keynote speaker and corporate consultant. During the course of his own successful career, he developed The MODERN Sales System, which he has been sharing with companies and associations around the world for many years.

A Certified Speaking Professional and a member of the National Speakers Association, Carl teaches essential sales skills with humor, insight and personal experience. Hundreds of companies throughout a diverse range of industries have used his highly-acclaimed seminars to educate and inspire their sales teams.

Carl's other books include The MODERN Sales System, 15 Hot Tips That Will Supercharge Your Sales Career, The PEOPLE Approach to Customer Service, Sell Something Everyday, 52 Things Every Sales Manager Needs to Know, and High Energy Sales Thoughts.

He currently lives in Charlotte, North Carolina.

To order additional copies of this book, or find out about Carl's seminars contact him at:

Henry Associates
704-847-7390
9430 Valley Road Charlotte, NC 28270
chenry@carlhenry.com
www.carlhenry.com

To order additional copies of this book contact:

Henry Associates
704-847-7390
9430 Valley Road Charlotte, NC 28270
chenry@carlhenry.com
www.carlhenry.com

Printed in the United States
212339BV00004B/5/P